Daily Reflections on Life's Great Truths

By
Larry John Phillips

No part of this publication may be reproduced, stored in a retrieval system, or transmitted in any form or by any means, electronic, mechanical, photocopying, recording, or otherwise, without the written permission of the publisher.

Text Copyright © 2024 Larry John Phillips

All rights reserved.
Published 2024 by Progressive Rising Phoenix Press, LLC
www.progressiverisingphoenix.com

ISBN: 978-1-958640-66-1

Printed in the U.S.A.
1st Printing

Illustrations: Shutterstock Image IDs: 1939947568 (Quotation Separator Flourish). Image used under license from Shutterstock.com.

Cover Photo: "Realistic Ripples on a Pond." Stock Photo ID: 2475841391 By ShutterStock AI Generator. Image used under license from ShutterStock.com.

Book and Cover design by Amanda M. Thrasher and William Speir
Visit: http://www.williamspeir.com

Daily Reflections on Life's Great Truths

January 1

I expect to spend the rest of my life in the future, so I want to be reasonably sure of what kind of future it's going to be. That is my reason for planning.
CHARLES F. KETTERING

Let him who would enjoy a good future waste none of the present.
ROGER BABSON

Notes:

Daily Reflections on Life's Great Truths

January
2

All worthwhile men have good thoughts, good ideas and good intentions – but precious few of them ever translate those into action.
J. H. FIELD

Well done is better than well said.
BENJAMIN FRANKLIN

Notes:
_____
_____
_____
_____
_____
_____
_____
_____
_____
_____
_____

Daily Reflections on Life's Great Truths

January 3

If we had no winter, the spring would not be so pleasant; if we did not sometimes taste adversity, prosperity would not be so welcome.
ANNE BRADSTREET

The diamond cannot be polished without friction, nor the man perfected without trials.
CHINESE PROVERB

Notes:

Daily Reflections on Life's Great Truths

January 4

In giving advice seek to help, not to please, your friend.
SOLON

When we are confronted with problems, the counsel of someone who has mastered similar problems can be of great help.
PANTANJALI

Notes:

Daily Reflections on Life's Great Truths

January 5

I love everything that is old: old friends, old times, old manners, old books, old wine.
OLIVER GOLDSMITH

Only years make men. Rarely do the great men of history distinguish themselves before they are fifty, and between fifty and eighty they do their best work – both as regards quality and quantity.
ADOLPH PHILIP GOUTHEY

Notes:

January 6

The people who are crazy enough to think they can change the world are the ones who do.
STEVE JOBS

There is one weakness in people for which there is no remedy. It is the universal weakness of lack of ambition.
NAPOLEON HILL

Notes:

Daily Reflections on Life's Great Truths

January 7

He that is slow to wrath is of great understanding: but he that is hasty of spirit exalteth folly.
BIBLE

How much more grievous are the consequences of anger than the causes of it.
MARCUS AURELIUS

Notes:

January 8

Do not look forward to what might happen tomorrow; the same Everlasting Father who cares for you today will take care of you tomorrow and every day. Either He will shield you from suffering, or He will give you unfailing strength to bear it. Be at peace then and put aside all anxious thoughts and imaginations.
FRANCIS DE SALES

Notes:

Daily Reflections on Life's Great Truths

January 9

Appearances do not make the man, but it will pay any man to make the best appearance possible.
ROY L. SMITH

Keeping your clothes well pressed will keep you from looking hard pressed.
COLEMAN COX

Notes:

Daily Reflections on Life's Great Truths

January 10

Don't be stingy with words of appreciation when they are justly due. Everyone likes to be told that he is admired, respected, and appreciated, and liked.
NICOLAS CAUSSIN

Someone who feels appreciated will do more than someone who is simply being paid.
J. S. FELTS

Notes:

Daily Reflections on Life's Great Truths

January
11

There is little difference in people, but that little difference makes a big difference. The little difference is attitude. The big difference is whether it is positive or negative.
W. CLEMENT STONE

Whether you think you can or whether you think you can't, you're right.
HENRY FORD

Notes:

Daily Reflections on Life's Great Truths

January 12

Though we travel the world over to find the beautiful, we must carry it within us, or we find it not.
RALPH WALDO EMERSON

Outer beauty turns the head, inner beauty turns the heart.
HELEN J. RUSSELL

Notes:

Daily Reflections on Life's Great Truths

January 13

Take, I pray thee, my blessing that is brought to thee; because God hath dealt graciously with me, and because I have enough.
BIBLE

There are two blessings which most people misuse - health and leisure.
MUHAMMAD

Notes:

Daily Reflections on Life's Great Truths

January 14

The first time I read an excellent book, it is to me just as if I had gained a new friend. When I read over a book I have perused before, it resembles the meeting with an old one.
OLIVER GOLDSMITH

In books we have the choicest thoughts of the ablest men in their best dress.
JOHN AIKIN

Notes:

Daily Reflections on Life's Great Truths

January 15

Nothing so bolsters our self-confidence and reconciles us with ourselves as the continuous ability to create; to see things grow and develop under our hand, day in, day out.
ERIC HOFFER

Fired by success – they could do it because they believed they could do it.
VIRGIL

Notes:

Daily Reflections on Life's Great Truths

January 16

A good conscience is a mine of wealth. And in truth what greater riches can there be, what thing more sweet than a good conscience.
ST. BERNARD

A peace above all earthly dignities, a still and quiet conscience.
WILLIAM SHAKESPEARE

Notes:

Daily Reflections on Life's Great Truths

January 17

Sweet are the thoughts that savor of content; the quiet mind is richer than a crown.
ROBERT GREENE

Then be content, poor heart! God's plans, like lilies pure and white, unfold; we must not tear the close-shut leaves apart. Time will reveal the calyxes of gold!
MARY LOUISE R. SMITH

Notes:

Daily Reflections on Life's Great Truths

January 18

Teamwork divides the task and multiplies the success.
ANONYMOUS

Together ordinary people can achieve extraordinary results.
BECKA SCHOETTLE

Notes:

Daily Reflections on Life's Great Truths

January

19

Do not pray for easy lives; pray to be stronger men.
Do not pray for tasks equal to your powers; pray for powers equal to your tasks.
PHILLIPS BROOKS

Courage starts with showing up and letting ourselves be seen.
BRENE BROWN

Notes:

Daily Reflections on Life's Great Truths

January 20

Really big people are, above everything else, courteous, considerate and generous – not just to some people in some circumstances – but to everyone all the time.
THOMAS J. WATSON

If a man be gracious and courteous to strangers, it shows he is a citizen of the world.
FRANCIS BACON

Notes:

Daily Reflections on Life's Great Truths

January 21

Imagination is the beginning of creation. You imagine what you desire, you will what you imagine, and at last, you create what you will.
GEORGE BERNARD SHAW

Creativity requires the courage to let go of certainties.
ERICH FROMM

Notes:

Daily Reflections on Life's Great Truths

January 22

One of the secrets of life is to keep our intellectual curiosity acute.
WILLIAM LYON PHELPS

The important thing is not to stop questioning. Curiosity has its own reason for existing.
ALBERT EINSTEIN

Notes:
_____
_____
_____
_____
_____
_____
_____
_____
_____
_____
_____
_____

Daily Reflections on Life's Great Truths

January 23

As a well-spent day brings happy sleep, so a life well spent brings happy death.
LEONARDO DA VINCI

The presence of death makes more meaningful all of the values of life.
JOSHUA LIEBMAN

Notes:

Daily Reflections on Life's Great Truths

January 24

More decisions are dictated by human feelings than are made by logic and reason.
DR. PAUL PARKER

Your capacity to say "NO" determines your capacity to say "YES" to greater things.
E. STANLEY JONES

Notes:

Daily Reflections on Life's Great Truths

January 25

Dependability is built over time. When people see that you keep your word, make careful promises, and work to correct mistakes, their trust and ability to depend on you will grow.
CHARACTER FIRST EDUCATION

It is worth everything to be dependable.
TODD W. VAN BECK

Notes:

Daily Reflections on Life's Great Truths

January
26

Failure will never overtake me, if my determination to succeed is strong enough.
OG MANDINO

If you set goals and go after them with all the determination you muster, your gifts will take you places that will amaze you.
LES BROWN

Notes:

Daily Reflections on Life's Great Truths

January
27

No horse gets anywhere until he is harnessed. No steam or gas ever drives anything until it is confined. No Niagara is ever turned into light and power until it is tunneled. No life ever grows great until it is focused, dedicated, disciplined.
HARRY EMERSON FOSDICK

It is the bridle and the spur that makes a good horse.
THOMAS FULLER

Notes:

Daily Reflections on Life's Great Truths

January
28

A man's mind, stretched by new ideas, may never return to its original dimensions.
OLIVER WENDELL HOLMES JR.

If you think education is expensive, try ignorance.
ANDY MCINTYRE

Notes:

Daily Reflections on Life's Great Truths

January
29

Let my heart be wise. It is the god's best gift.
EURIPIDES

Seeing's believing, but feeling's the truth.
THOMAS FULLER

Notes:

Daily Reflections on Life's Great Truths

January 30

Flaming enthusiasm, backed up by horse sense and persistence, is the quality that most frequently makes for success.
DALE CARNEGIE

Knowledge is power, but enthusiasm pulls the switch.
IVERN BALL

Notes:

Daily Reflections on Life's Great Truths

January
31

All of us do not have equal talent, but all of us should have an equal opportunity to develop our talents.
JOHN F. KENNEDY

We will never have true civilization until we have learned to recognize the rights of others.
WILL ROGERS

Notes:

Daily Reflections on Life's Great Truths

February 1

Ethics is knowing the difference between what you have a right to do and what is right to do.
POTTER STEWART

In law, a man is guilty when he violates the rights of others. In ethics, he is guilty if he only thinks of doing so.
IMMANUEL KANT

Notes:

Daily Reflections on Life's Great Truths

February 2

Physical fitness is not only one of the most important keys to a healthy body, it is the basis of dynamic and creative intellectual activity.
JOHN F. KENNEDY

Walking is the best possible exercise. Habituate yourself to walk very far.
THOMAS JEFFERSON

Notes:

Daily Reflections on Life's Great Truths

February 3

Experience keeps a dear school, but fools will learn in no other.
BENJAMIN FRANKLIN

One thorn of experience is worth a whole wilderness of warning.
JAMES RUSSELL LOWELL

Notes:

Daily Reflections on Life's Great Truths

February 4

Fear knocked at the door and faith answered. No one was there.
OLD ENGLISH PROVERB

There are only two ways to live...one is as though nothing is a miracle...the other is as if everything is.
ALBERT EINSTEIN

Notes:

Daily Reflections on Life's Great Truths

February 5

We may have our differences, but nothing's more important than family.
COCO

To us, family means putting your arms around each other and being there.
BARBARA BUSH

Notes:

Daily Reflections on Life's Great Truths

February 6

Forgiveness does not mean ignoring what has been done or putting a false label on an evil act. It means, rather, that the evil act no longer remains as a barrier to the relationship. Forgiveness is a catalyst creating the atmosphere necessary for a fresh start and a new beginning.
MARTIN LUTHER KING, JR.

Notes:

Daily Reflections on Life's Great Truths

February 7

Is freedom anything else than the right to live as we wish? Nothing else.
EPICTETUS

∽

No one outside ourselves can rule us inwardly. When we know this, we become free.
BUDDHA

Notes:
_____
_____
_____
_____
_____
_____
_____
_____
_____
_____
_____
_____

February 8

Don't walk in front of me, I may not follow; Don't walk behind, I may not lead; Walk beside me, and just be my friend.
ALBERT CAMUS

Friendship is a strong and habitual inclination in two persons to promote the good and happiness of another.
EUSTANCE BUDGELL

Notes:

Daily Reflections on Life's Great Truths

February 9

There is no dignity quite so impressive, and no independence quite so important, as living within your means.
CALVIN COOLIDGE

He who will not economize will have to agonize.
CONFUCIUS

Notes:

Daily Reflections on Life's Great Truths

February 10

The man least dependent upon the morrow goes to meet the morrow most cheerfully.
EPICURUS

He that fears not the future may enjoy the present.
THOMAS FULLER

Notes:

Daily Reflections on Life's Great Truths

February 11

Always give without remembering and always receive without forgetting.
BRIAN TRACY

We make a living by what we get. We make a life by what we give.
WINSTON CHURCHILL

Notes:

Daily Reflections on Life's Great Truths

February

12

Nothing is so strong as gentleness, nothing so gentle as real strength.
FRANCIS DE SALES

In a gentle way, you can shake the world.
MAHATMA GANDHI

Notes:

Daily Reflections on Life's Great Truths

February 13

How happy a person is depends upon the depth of his gratitude. You will notice at once that the unhappy person has little gratitude toward life, other people, and God.
JOHN MILLER

Ingratitude is always a kind of weakness. I have never known men of ability to be ungrateful.
JOHANN WOLFGANG VON GOETHE

Notes:

Daily Reflections on Life's Great Truths

February 14

All love that has not friendship for its base, is like a mansion built upon the sand.
ELLA WHEELER WILCOX

We are most alive when we're in love.
JOHN UPDIKE

Notes:

Daily Reflections on Life's Great Truths

February 15

Successful people aren't born that way. They become successful by establishing the habits of doing things unsuccessful people don't like to do.
WILLIAM MAKEPEACE THACKERAY

～

We are what we repeatedly do. Excellence then, is not an act, but a habit.
WILL DURANT

Notes:

Daily Reflections on Life's Great Truths

February

16

Happiness depends, on as nature shows, less on exterior things than most suppose.
WILLIAM COWPER

It is not how much we have, but how much we enjoy, that makes happiness.
CLAIRE BOOTHE SPURGEON

Notes:

Daily Reflections on Life's Great Truths

February

17

Without health all men are poor.
ANONYMOUS

A healthy outside starts from the inside.
ROBERT URICH

Notes:

Daily Reflections on Life's Great Truths

February 18

A comfortable house is a great source of happiness. It ranks immediately after health and a good conscience.
SYDNEY SMITH

People are usually the happiest at home.
WILLIAM SHAKESPEARE

Notes:

Daily Reflections on Life's Great Truths

February
19

I hope I shall possess firmness and virtue enough to maintain what I consider the most enviable of all titles, the character of an honest man.
GEORGE WASHINGTON

❧

No legacy is so rich as honesty.
WILLIAM SHAKESPEARE

Notes:

February 20

From our ancestors come our names, from our virtues our honors.
ANONYMOUS

Honor has not to be won; it must only not be lost.
ARTHUR SCHOPENHAUER

Notes:

Daily Reflections on Life's Great Truths

February 21

The work goes on, the cause endures, the hope still lives, and the dreams shall never die.
EDWARD KENNEDY

Be prepared, work hard, and hope for a little luck. Recognize that the harder you work and the better prepared you are, the more luck you might have.
ED BRADLEY

Notes:

Daily Reflections on Life's Great Truths

February
22

The reward for humility and fear of the Lord is riches and honour and life.
BIBLE

The proud man counts his newspaper clippings, the humble his blessings.
FULTON J. SHEEN

Notes:

February 23

Good humor is a tonic for mind and body. It is the best antidote for anxiety and depression. It is a business asset. It attracts and keeps friends. It lightens human burdens. It is the direct route to serenity and contentment.
GRENVILLE KLEISER

Notes:

Daily Reflections on Life's Great Truths

February 24

Life without liberty is like a body without spirit.
KAHLIL GIBRAN

I am no bird; and no net ensnares me; I am a free human being with an independent will.
JANE EYRE

Notes:
___
___
___
___
___
___
___
___
___
___
___
___
___

February 25

A smart man makes a mistake, learns from it, and never makes that mistake again. But a wise man finds a smart man and learns from him how to avoid the mistake altogether.
ROY WILLIAMS

Talent hits a target no one else can hit; genius hits a target no one else can see.
ARTHUR SCHOPENHAUER

Notes:

February 26

To give every man his due, that is supreme justice.
MARCUS TULLIUS CICERO

Of all the things of a man's soul which he has within him, justice is the greatest good and injustice the greatest evil.
PLATO

Notes:

Daily Reflections on Life's Great Truths

February 27

Be kind, for everyone you meet is fighting a battle you know nothing about.
WENDY MASS

Never lose a chance of saying a kind word.
WILLIAM MAKEPEACE THACKERAY

Notes:

Daily Reflections on Life's Great Truths

February 28/29

The saying that knowledge is power is not quite true. Used knowledge is power, and more than power. It is money, and service, and better living for our fellowmen, and a hundred other good things. But mere knowledge, let unused, has no power in it.
DR. EDWARD E. FREE

Notes:

Daily Reflections on Life's Great Truths

March 1

What we do during our working hours determines what we have, what we do in our leisure hours determines what we are.
GEORGE EASTMAN

What the banker sighs for, the meanest clown may have, - leisure and a quiet mind.
HENRY DAVID THOREAU

Notes:

March 2

A man can do nothing better than to eat and drink and find satisfaction in his work.
BIBLE

The journey, not the arrival, matters; the voyage, not the landing.
LOUIS THEROUX

Notes:

March 3

You cannot buy loyalty. You cannot buy the devotion of hearts, minds, and souls. You have to earn these things.
CLARENCE FRANCIS

True loyalty is proven, not proclaimed.
GRAIG GROESCHEL

Notes:

Daily Reflections on Life's Great Truths

March 4

If you want to pull yourself into a glorious adulthood and personal fulfillment, do not permit yourself to live an uncharted life.
RHODA LACHAR

When I was a child, I spake as a child, I understood as a child, I thought as a child; but when I became a man, I put away childish things.
BIBLE

Notes:

Daily Reflections on Life's Great Truths

March 5

I will not be a slave to myself, for it is a perpetual, a shameful, and the most heavy of all servitudes; and this end I may gain by moderate desires.
LUCIUS ANNAEUS SENECA

It is circumstance and proper measure that give an action its character, and make it either good or bad.
PLUTARCH

Notes:

Daily Reflections on Life's Great Truths

March 6

All that is really useful to us can be bought for little money; it is only the superfluous that is put up for sale at a high price.
AXEL MUNTHE

An inheritance quickly gained at the beginning will not be blessed at the end.
BIBLE

Notes:

Daily Reflections on Life's Great Truths

March 7

Choose to be an optimist. It feels better.
DALAI LAMA

It is the hopeful, buoyant, cheerful attitude of mind that wins. Optimism is a success builder; pessimism an achievement killer.
ORISON SWETT MARDEN

Notes:

Daily Reflections on Life's Great Truths

March 8

For every minute spent in organizing, an hour is earned.
BENJAMIN FRANKLIN

Organize your life around your dreams, and watch them come true.
ANONYMOUS

Notes:

March 9

Trust God to weave your thread into the great web, though the pattern shows it not yet.
GEORGE MACDONALD

Adopt the pace of nature; her secret is patience.
RALPH WALDO EMERSON

Notes:

Daily Reflections on Life's Great Truths

March 10

Resign every forbidden joy; restrain every wish that is not referred to God's will; banish all eager desires, all anxiety; desire only the will of God; seek him alone and supremely, and you will find peace.
FRANCOIS FENELON

Nothing can disturb your peace of mind unless you allow.
ROY T. BENNETT

Notes:

Daily Reflections on Life's Great Truths

March 11

With ordinary talent and extraordinary perseverance, all things are attainable.
SIR THOMAS FOXWELL BUXTON

Victory belongs to the most persevering.
NAPOLEON BONAPARTE

Notes:

Daily Reflections on Life's Great Truths

March
12

Keep on going, and the chances are that you will stumble on something, perhaps when you are least expecting it. I never heard of anyone ever stumbling on something sitting down.
CHARLES F. KETTERING

Our glory is not in never failing, but in rising up every time we fail.
RALPH WALDO EMERSON

Notes:

Daily Reflections on Life's Great Truths

March 13

The love of pleasure is one of the great elementary instincts of human nature.
ARISTOTLE

Variety is the soul of pleasure.
APHRA BEHN

Notes:

March 14

It is the preoccupation with possessions, more than anything else, that prevents us from living freely and nobly.
BERTRAND RUSSELL

Once you need less, you'll have more.
ANONYMOUS

Notes:

Daily Reflections on Life's Great Truths

March 15

Live for something, have a purpose, and keep that purpose in view.
ROBERT WHITAKER

Nothing will divert me from my purpose.
ABRAHAM LINCOLN

Notes:

March 16

Character is like a tree and reputation like its shadow. The shadow is what we think of it; the tree is the real thing.
ABRAHAM LINCOLN

Your reputation is in the hands of others. That's what reputation is. You can't control that. The only thing you can control is your character.
WAYNE W. DYER

Notes:

Daily Reflections on Life's Great Truths

March 17

We should all consider each other as human beings, and we should respect each other.
MALALA YOUSAFZAI

Most good relationships are built on mutual trust and respect.
MONA SUTPHEN

Notes:

Daily Reflections on Life's Great Truths

March 18

Responsibility is the thing people dread most of all. Yet it is the one thing in the world that develops us, gives us manhood or womanhood fibre.
FRANK CRANE

༄

You must create your own world. I am responsible for my world.
LOUISE NEVELSON

Notes:

Daily Reflections on Life's Great Truths

March 19

Retire from your job, but never retire your mind.
ANONYMOUS

I see retirement as just another of these reinventions, another chance to do new things and be a new version of myself.
WALT MOSSBERG

Notes:

March 20

A man of knowledge uses words with restraint, and a man of understanding is even-tempered.
BIBLE

A man who lives right, and is right, has more power in his silence than another has by his words.
PHILLIPS BROOKS

Notes:

Daily Reflections on Life's Great Truths

March 21

Simplicity, simplicity, simplicity! I say, let your affairs be as two or three, and not a hundred or a thousand; instead of a million count half a dozen, and keep your accounts on your thumb-nail.
HENRY DAVID THOREAU

To be simple is to be great.
RALPH WALDO EMERSON

Notes:

March 22

Never has there been one possessed of complete sincerity who did not move others. Never has there been one who had not sincerity who was able to move others.
MENCIUS

Sincerity may not help us make friends, but it will help us keep them.
JOHN WOODEN

Notes:

Daily Reflections on Life's Great Truths

March

23

It is only in solitude that I ever find my own core.
ANNE MORROW LINDBERGH

Converse with men makes sharp the glittering wit,
but God to man doth speak in solitude.
JOHN STUART BLACKIE

Notes:

Daily Reflections on Life's Great Truths

March

24

The great thing in this world is not so much where we stand as in what direction we are moving.
OLIVER WENDELL HOLMES

Success consists of going from failure to failure without loss of enthusiasm.
WINSTON CHURCHILL

Notes:

Daily Reflections on Life's Great Truths

March 25

Take this sorrow to thy heart, and make it a part of thee, and it shall nourish thee till thou are strong again.
HENRY WADSWORTH LONGFELLOW

We are healed of suffering only by experiencing it to the full.
MARCEL PROUST

Notes:

March 26

Talent without working hard is nothing.
ANONYMOUS

If a man can write a better book, preach a better sermon, or make a better mouse-trap, than his neighbor, though he builds his house in the woods, the world will make a beaten path to his door.
RALPH WALDO EMERSON

Notes:

Daily Reflections on Life's Great Truths

March 27

We are what our thoughts have made us, so take care about what you think. Words are secondary. Thoughts live, they travel far.
SWAMI VIVEKANANDA

All that we are is the result of what we have thought.
BUDDHA

Notes:
_____
_____
_____
_____
_____
_____
_____
_____
_____
_____
_____
_____
_____

March 28

You wake up in the morning, and lo! Your purse is magically filled with twenty-four hours of the unmanufactured tissue of the universe of your life. It is yours. It is the most precious of possessions. No one can take it from you. It is unstealable. And no one receives more or less than you receive.
ARNOLD BENNETT

Notes:

March 29

Tolerance isn't about not having beliefs. It's about how your beliefs lead you to treat people who disagree with you.
TIMOTHY KELLER

I do not like what you say but I will defend to the death your right to say it.
VOLTAIRE

Notes:

March 30

The most important lesson that I learned is to trust God in every circumstance. Lots of times we go through difficult trials and following God's plan seems like it doesn't make any sense at all. God is always in control and he will never leave us.
ALLYSON FELIX

Notes:

Daily Reflections on Life's Great Truths

March 31

The price of wisdom is above rubies.
BIBLE

The beginning of wisdom is to call things by their right names.
CHINESE PROVERB

Notes:

Daily Reflections on Life's Great Truths

April 1

Work expands so as to fill the time available for its completion.
C. NORTHCOTE PARKINSON

Work keeps from three great evils: boredom, vice, and want.
VOLTAIRE

Notes:

Daily Reflections on Life's Great Truths

April 2

TSZE-KUNG asked what constituted a superior man. The Master said, "He acts before he speaks, and afterwards speaks according to his actions."
CONFUCIUS

If I rest, I rust.
ALDOUS HUXLEY

Notes:

Daily Reflections on Life's Great Truths

April 3

Adversity reveals and shapes character.
ANONYMOUS

He knows not the value of a day of pleasure who has not seen adversity.
SA'DI

Notes:

Daily Reflections on Life's Great Truths

April 4

Get the advice of everybody whose advice is worth having-they are very few-and then do what you think best yourself.
CHARLES STEWART PARNELL

The way of a fool seems right to him, but a wise man listens to advice.
BIBLE

Notes:

April 5

The older I get, the greater power I seem to have to help the world; I am like a snowball – the further I am rolled, the more I gain.
SUSAN B. ANTHONY

To me, old age is always fifteen year older than I am.
BERNARD M. BARUGH

Notes:

April 6

The successful man has ambition: before an engine has any power, it must have a fire under the boilers. Ambition was the fire that stirred Edison, Lindbergh, and other successful men who have been more interested in achievement than in public applause.
A. B. ZU TAVERN

Notes:

Daily Reflections on Life's Great Truths

April 7

A soft answer turneth away wrath; but grievous words stir up anger.
BIBLE

How many a day has been saddened and darkened by an angry word.
JOHN LUBBOCK

Notes:

April 8

Anxiety is the rust of life, destroying its brightness and weakening its power. A childlike and abiding trust in Providence is its best preventative and remedy.
TRYON EDWARDS

Anxiety is the interest paid on trouble before it is due.
DEAN WILLIAM R. INGE

Notes:

April 9

It's not the garb he wears that makes the monk.
BLAISE PASCAL

Outside show is a poor substitute for inner worth.
AESOP

Notes:

Daily Reflections on Life's Great Truths

April 10

Make it a habit to tell people thank you. To express your appreciation, sincerely and without the expectation of anything in return. Truly appreciate those around you, and you'll soon find many others around you. Truly appreciate life, and you'll find that you have more of it.
RALPH MARSTON

Notes:
_____
_____
_____
_____
_____
_____
_____
_____
_____
_____
_____

April 11

If you don't like something, change it. If you can't change it, change your attitude.
MAYA ANGELOU

No matter what happens in your life, find the good. Your attitude can be either positive or negative. The choice is up to you.
CATHERINE PULSIFER

Notes:

Daily Reflections on Life's Great Truths

April 12

Take care of your inner, spiritual beauty. That will reflect in your face.
DOLORES DEL RIO

Beauty is when you can appreciate yourself. When you love yourself, that's when you're most beautiful.
ZOE KRAVITZ

Notes:

Daily Reflections on Life's Great Truths

April 13

The best things are nearest: breath in your nostrils, light in your eyes, flowers at your feet, duties at your hand, the path of God just before you. Then do not grasp at the stars, but do life's plain, common work as it comes, certain that daily duties and daily bread are the sweetest things in life.
ROBERT LOUIS STEVENSON

Notes:

Daily Reflections on Life's Great Truths

April 14

A book by its counsel teaches a wise man how to live.
PHAEDRUS

Books, like friends should be few and well chosen.
KEVIN PATTERSON

Notes:

Daily Reflections on Life's Great Truths

April 15

It's not the strongest species that survives, nor the most intelligent, but the most responsive to change.
CHARLES DARWIN

Everyone wants to live on top of the mountain, but all the happiness and growth occurs while you're climbing it.
ANDY ROONEY

Notes:

Daily Reflections on Life's Great Truths

April 16

Man becomes calm in the measure that he understands himself as a thought-evolved being.
JAMES ALLEN

Calmness is the rarest quality in human life. It is the poise of a great nature, in harmony with itself and its ideals.
WILLIAM G. GORDON

Notes:

Daily Reflections on Life's Great Truths

April 17

Caring about others, running the risk of feeling, and leaving an impact on people brings happiness.
HAROLD KUSHNER

Never be So busy as not to think of others.
MOTHER TERESA

Notes:

Daily Reflections on Life's Great Truths

April 18

A wise man changes his mind, a fool never.
SPANISH PROVERB

The world hates change, yet it is the only thing that has bought progress.
CHARLES F. KETTERING

Notes:

Daily Reflections on Life's Great Truths

April 19

The greatest legacy one can pass to one's children and grandchildren is not money or other material things accumulated in one's life, but rather a legacy of character and faith.
BILLY GRAHAM

Talents are best nurtured in solitude. Character is best formed in the stormy billows of the world.
JOHANN WOLFGANG VON GOETHE

Notes:

April 20

The most certain sign of wisdom is cheerfulness.
MICHEL DE MONTAIGNE

You find yourself refreshed in the presence of cheerful people. Why not make an honest effort to confer that pleasure on others?
LYDIA M. CHILD

Notes:

April 21

Nothing ranks a man so quickly as his skill in selecting things that are really worthwhile. Every day brings the necessity of keen discrimination. Not always is it a choice between good and bad, but between good and best.
ADOLPH PHILIP GOUTHEY

Notes:

April 22

Circumstances do not make a man; they only reveal him to himself.
JAMES ALLEN

Circumstances may prevent you from building a fortune, but they have no power to prevent you from building character.
ARISTOTLE

Notes:

April 23

Cleanliness is indeed next to godliness.
JOHN WESLEY

Neatness and cleanliness is not a function of how rich or poor you are but that of mentality and principle.
IKECHUKWU IZUAKOR

Notes:

Daily Reflections on Life's Great Truths

April 24

Compassion is the greatest form of love humans have to offer.
RACHAEL JOY SCOTT

We can't heal the world today, but we can begin with a voice of compassion, a heart of love, an act of kindness.
MARY DAVIS

Notes:

April 25

The virtue of man ought to be measured, not by his extraordinary exertions, but by his everyday conduct.
BLAISE PASCAL

Depend not on fortune, but on conduct.
PUBLILIUS SYRUS

Notes:

Daily Reflections on Life's Great Truths

April 26

Your success depends mainly upon what you think of yourself and whether you believe in yourself.
WILLIAM J. H. BOETCKER

The man who cannot believe in himself cannot believe in anything else.
ROY L. SMITH

Notes:

Daily Reflections on Life's Great Truths

April 27

Wrong does not cease to be wrong because the majority share in it.
LEO TOLSTOY

Keep conscience clear, then never fear.
BENJAMIN FRANKLIN

Notes:

Daily Reflections on Life's Great Truths

April 28

He is not rich that possesses much, but he that is content with what he has.
ANONYMOUS

He who has fewest wants, and is most able to live within himself, is not only the happiest, but the richest man, and if he does not abound in what the world calls wealth, he does in independence.
ANONYMOUS

Notes:

April 29

Cooperation doesn't mean agreement, it means working together to advance the greater good.
SIMON SINEK

Nothing truly valuable can be achieved except by the unselfish cooperation of many individuals.
ALBERT EINSTEIN

Notes:

April 30

Life shrinks or expands in proportion to one's courage.
ANAIS NIN

I do not ask to walk smooth paths nor bear an easy load. I pray for strength and fortitude to climb the rock-strewn road. Give me such courage I can scale the hardest peaks alone, and transform every stumbling block into a steppingstone.
GAIL BROOK BURKET

Notes:

Daily Reflections on Life's Great Truths

May 1

Many men fail because they do not see the importance of being kind and courteous to the men under them. Kindness to everybody always pays for itself. And besides, it is a pleasure to be kind.
CHARLES M. SCHWAB

Nothing is gained by not being kind and courteous.
NEAL ADAMS

Notes:

May 2

> Imagination rules the world.
> NAPOLEON BONAPARTE

> Curiosity about life in all aspects, I think, is still the secret of great creative people.
> LEO BURNETT

Notes:

Daily Reflections on Life's Great Truths

May 3

Knowing the answers will help you in school.
Knowing how to question will help you in life.
WARREN BERGER

I have no special talents. I am only passionately curious.
ALBERT EINSTEIN

Notes:

Daily Reflections on Life's Great Truths

May 4

I often feel that death is not the enemy of life, but its friend, for knowledge that our years are limited which makes them so precious.
JOSHUA LIEBMAN

It matters not how a man dies, but how he lives. The act of dying is not of importance, it lasts so short of time.
SAMUEL JOHNSON

Notes:

May 5

When confronted with two courses of action, I jot down on a piece of paper all the arguments in favor of each one – then, on the opposite side, I write the arguments against each one. Then by weighing the arguments, pro and con, and canceling them out, one against the other, I take the course indicated by what remains.
BENJAMIN FRANKLIN

Notes:

Daily Reflections on Life's Great Truths

May 6

The more dependable and resourceful we are, the more respect we command and deserve from our superiors and fellow employees alike.
TODD W. VAN BECK

Ability is important in our quest for success, but dependability is critical.
ZIG ZIGLAR

Notes:

Daily Reflections on Life's Great Truths

May 7

Desire is the key to motivation, but it's determination and commitment to an unrelenting pursuit of your goal – a commitment to excellence – that will enable you to attain the success you seek.
MARIO ANDRETTI

The difference between the impossible and possible lies in a man's determination.
TOMMY LASORDA

Notes:

Daily Reflections on Life's Great Truths

May
8

No discipline seems pleasant at the time, but painful. Later on, however, it produces a harvest of righteousness and peace for those who have been trained by it.
BIBLE

That aim in life is highest, which requires the highest and finest discipline.
HENRY DAVID THOREAU

Notes:

Daily Reflections on Life's Great Truths

May 9

If a man empties his purse into his head, no man can take it away from him. An investment in knowledge always pays the best interest.
BENJAMIN FRANKLIN

Apply yourself. Get all the education you can, but then, by God, do something. Don't just stand there, make it happen.
LEE IACOCCA

Notes:

May 10

Reason guides but a small part of man, and that the least interesting. The rest obeys feeling, true or false, and passion, good or bad.
JOSEPH ROUX

Whatever makes an impression on the heart seems lovely in the eye.
SA'DI

Notes:

Daily Reflections on Life's Great Truths

May 11

Years wrinkle the face, but to give up enthusiasm wrinkles the soul.
WATTERSON LOWE

The secret of genius is to carry the spirit of the child into old age, which means never losing your enthusiasm.
ALDOUS HUXLEY

Notes:

Daily Reflections on Life's Great Truths

May 12

They who say all men are equal speak an undoubted truth, if they mean all that have an equal right to liberty, to their property, and to their protection of the laws. But they are mistaken if they think men are equal in their station and employments, since they are not so by their talents.
VOLTAIRE

Notes:

Daily Reflections on Life's Great Truths

May 13

A gentleman takes as much trouble to discover what is right as the lesser men take to discover what will pay.
CONFUCIUS

Most people are willing to take the Sermon on the Mount as a flag to sail under; but few will use is as a rudder by which to steer.
OLIVER WENDELL HOLMES

Notes:

Daily Reflections on Life's Great Truths

May 14

A vigorous five-mile walk will do more good for an unhappy but otherwise healthy adult than all the medicine and psychology in the world.
PAUL DUDLEY WHITE

Those who think they have not time for bodily exercise will sooner or later have to find time for illness.
EDWARD STANLEY

Notes:

Daily Reflections on Life's Great Truths

May 15

Is there anyone so wise as to learn by the experience of others?
VOLTAIRE

Experience is a good school. But the fees are high.
HEINRICH HEINE

Notes:

Daily Reflections on Life's Great Truths

May 16

Faith is staying focused on the positive and being grateful for what you have. Faith is trusting that the right answer to a problem will come to you – it's waiting patiently until things get resolved – knowing that prayer can be answered in many ways. All I have seen teaches me to trust the Creator for all I have not seen.
ANONYMOUS

Notes:

Daily Reflections on Life's Great Truths

May 17

Family gives you the roots to stand tall and strong.
ANONYMOUS

The most important thing in the world is family and love.
JOHN WOODEN

Notes:

Daily Reflections on Life's Great Truths

May 18

When a deep injury is done us, we never recover until we forgive.
ALAN PATON

Sins cannot be undone, only forgiven.
IGOR STRAVINSKY

Notes:

Daily Reflections on Life's Great Truths

May 19

I prefer liberty with danger than peace with slavery.
JEAN-JACQUES ROUSSEAU

When we lose the right to be different, we lose the privilege to be free.
CHARLES EVANS

Notes:

May 20

I keep my friends as misers do their treasures, because, of all the things granted us by wisdom, none is greater or better than friendship.
PIETRO ARETINO

If a man does not make new acquaintances as he advances through life, he will soon find himself alone. A man, sir, must keep his friendships in constant repair.
SAMUEL JOHNSON

Notes:

Daily Reflections on Life's Great Truths

May 21

Do not save what is left after spending, but spend what is left after saving.
WARREN BUFFETT

If you buy things you do not need, soon you will have to sell things you need.
WARREN BUFFETT

Notes:

Daily Reflections on Life's Great Truths

May 22

The future belongs to those who believe in the beauty of their dreams.
ELEANOR ROOSEVELT

What we do today will determine your future.
CATHERINE PULSIFER

Notes:

Daily Reflections on Life's Great Truths

May 23

Remember that the happiest people are not those getting more, but those giving more.
ROBIN SHARMA

To do more for the world than the world does for you – that is success.
HENRY FORD

Notes:

Daily Reflections on Life's Great Truths

May 24

In the long run, the sharpest weapon of all is a kind and gentle spirit.
ANNE FRANK

Only the gentle are ever really strong.
JAMES DEAN

Notes:

May 25

That is not more pleasing exercise of the mind than gratitude.
JOSEPH ADDISON

Thou hast given so much to me...Give one more thing, a grateful heart.
GEORGE HERBERT

Notes:

Daily Reflections on Life's Great Truths

May 26

Each year one vicious habit discarded, in time might make the worst of us good.
BENJAMIN FRANKLIN

You'll never change your life until you change something you do daily. The secret of your success is found in your daily routine.
JOHN MAXWELL

Notes:

Daily Reflections on Life's Great Truths

May 27

Be happy with what you have and are, be generous with both, and you won't have to hunt for happiness.
WILLIAM E. GLADSTONE

The art of being happy lies in the power of extracting happiness from common things.
HENRY WARD BEECHER

Notes:

Daily Reflections on Life's Great Truths

May 28

Health is not valued till sickness comes.
THOMAS FULLER

Take care of your body. It's the only place you have to live.
JIM ROHN

Notes:

Daily Reflections on Life's Great Truths

May 29

No matter how big you are, when you go back home, your family treats you like a normal person.
AJITH KUMAR

There is nothing like staying at home for real comfort.
JANE AUSTEN

Notes:

Daily Reflections on Life's Great Truths

May
30

Being honest may not get you a lot of friends, but it'll always get you the right ones.
JOHN LENNON

The first step toward greatness is to be honest.
PROVERB

Notes:

Daily Reflections on Life's Great Truths

May 31

What is left when honor is lost?
PUBLILIUS SYRUS

Show me the man you honor, and I will know what kind of man you are.
THOMAS CARLYLE

Notes:

Daily Reflections on Life's Great Truths

June 1

Hope is important because it can make the present moment less difficult to bear. If we believe that tomorrow will be better, we can bear a hardship today.
THICH NHAT HANH

All human wisdom is summed up in two words, wait and hope.
ALEXANDER DUMAS

Notes:

June 2

The greater you are, the more you must practice humility.
BEN SIRA

Whoever exalts himself will be humbled, and whoever humbles himself will be exalted.
BIBLE

Notes:

Daily Reflections on Life's Great Truths

June 3

Among those whom I like or admire, I can find no common denominator, but among those whom I love, I can: all of them make me laugh.
W. H. AUDEN

A person without a sense of humor is like a wagon without springs. It's jolted by every pebble on the road.
HENRY WARD BEECHER

Notes:

Daily Reflections on Life's Great Truths

June 4

To find yourself, think for yourself.
SOCRATES

Don't let the noise of other's opinions drown out your own inner voice.
STEVE JOBS

Notes:

Daily Reflections on Life's Great Truths

June 5

If we encounter a man of rare intellect, we should ask him what books he reads.
RALPH WALDO EMERSON

Common sense is genius dressed in its working clothes.
RALPH WALDO EMERSON

Notes:

June 6

> By the just, we mean that which is lawful and that which is fair and equitable.
> ARISTOTLE

> If we do not maintain justice, justice will not maintain us.
> FRANCIS BACON

Notes:

June 7

In a world where you can be anything, be kind.
CLARE POOLEY

Kind words promote peace in our thoughts and our lives.
ALLENE VANOIRCHOT

Notes:

Daily Reflections on Life's Great Truths

June 8

The desire for knowledge, like the thirst of riches,
increases ever with the acquisition of it.
LAURENCE STERNE

It is not a question how much a man knows, but what
use he can make of what he knows.
JOSIAH GILBERT HOLLAND

Notes:

June 9

Leisure, some degree of it, is necessary to the health of every man's spirit.
HARRIET MARTINEAU

He does not seem to me to be a free man who does not sometimes do nothing.
MARCUS TULLIUS CICERO

Notes:

Daily Reflections on Life's Great Truths

June 10

The quality of a life is determined by its activities.
ARISTOTLE

The unexamined life is not worth living.
SOCRATES

Notes:

June 11

There is only one happiness in this life, to love and be loved.
GEORGE SAND

To love is nothing. To be loved is something. But to love and be loved, that's everything.
THEMIS TOLIS

Notes:

June 12

Loyalty means giving me your honest opinion, whether you think I'll like it or not.
COLIN POWELL

Loyalty to the Nation all the time, loyalty to the Government when it deserves it.
MARK TWAIN

Notes:

Daily Reflections on Life's Great Truths

June 13

Maturity is achieved when a person postpones immediate pleasures for long-term values.
JOSHUA L. LIEBMAN

Most of us don't mind doing what we ought to do when it doesn't interfere with what we want to do, but it takes discipline and maturity to do what we ought to do whether we want to or not.
JOSEPH B. WIRTHLIN

Notes:

Daily Reflections on Life's Great Truths

June 14

It may seem paradoxical, but it is certainly true, that in the long run, the moderate man will derive more enjoyment even from eating and drinking than the glutton or the drunkard will ever obtain.
JOHN LUBBOCK

Moderation is the inseparable companion to wisdom.
CHARLES CALEB COLTON

Notes:

Daily Reflections on Life's Great Truths

June 15

Always keep accounts, and keep them carefully. Keep them so that you know how the money goes and how much things cost you. No man who knows what his income is, and what he is spending, will run into extravagance.
JOHN LUBBOCK

As far as you can possibly, pay ready money for everything you buy, and avoid bills.
EARL OF CHESTERFIELD

Notes:

June 16

I am an optimist...I choose to be. There is a lot of darkness in our world, there is a lot of pain, and you can choose to see that, or you can choose to see the joy. If you try to respond positively to the world, you will spend your time better.
TOM HIDDLESTON

While we may not be able to control all that happens to us, we can control what happens inside us.
BENJAMIN FRANKLIN

Notes:

Daily Reflections on Life's Great Truths

June 17

A place for everything and everything in its place.
BENJAMIN FRANKLIN

Organization isn't about perfection; it's about efficiency, reducing stress and clutter, saving time and money, and improving overall quality of life.
CHRISTINA SCALISE

Notes:

June 18

It is not necessary for all men to be great in action. The greatest and sublimest power is often simple patience
HORACE BUSHNELL

No great thing is created suddenly, more than a bunch of grapes or a fig. If you tell me that you desire a fig, I answer you that there must be time. Let it first blossom, then bear fruit, then ripen.
EPICTETUS

Notes:

Daily Reflections on Life's Great Truths

June 19

Set peace of mind as your highest goal and organize your life around it.
ANONYMOUS

You'll never find peace of mind until you listen to your heart.
GEORGE MICHAEL

Notes:

Daily Reflections on Life's Great Truths

June 20

If you wish to succeed in life, make perseverance your bosom friend.
JOSEPH ADDISON

No one succeeds without effort...Those who succeed owe their success to their perseverance.
RAMANA MAHARSHI

Notes:

Daily Reflections on Life's Great Truths

June 21

Difficult things take a long time, impossible things a little longer.
ANONYMOUS

Success seems to be largely a matter of hanging in after others have let go.
WILLIAM FEATHER

Notes:

June 22

Most men that do thrive in the world do forget to take pleasure during the time that they are getting their estate, but reserve that till they have got one and then it is too late for them to enjoy it.
SAMUEL PEPYS

Business before pleasure.
ENGLISH SAYING

Notes:

June 23

Own less, love more.
JOSHUA BECKER

People who live below their expectations, enjoy a freedom people who are busy upgrading their lifestyles can't afford.
NAVAL RAVIKANT

Notes:

Daily Reflections on Life's Great Truths

June 24

There is one quality which one must possess to win, and that is definiteness of purpose, the knowledge of what one wants, and a burning desire to possess it.
NAPOLEON HILL

If you want to know what your purpose is, it is to make the most of your talents and skills for the greater good, and that means starting with yourself.
TONY CLARK

Notes:

June 25

Reputation is like fine china: Once broken it's very hard to repair.
ABRAHAM LINCOLN

Regard your good name as the richest jewel you can possibly be possessed of.
SOCRATES

Notes:

June 26

The final test of a gentleman is his respect for those who can be of no possible service to him.
WILLIAM LYON PHELPS

That you may retain your self-respect, it is better to displease the people by doing what you know is right, than to temporarily please them by doing what you know is wrong.
WILLIAM J. H. BOETCKER

Notes:

Daily Reflections on Life's Great Truths

June 27

Life always gets harder toward the summit – the cold increases, responsibility increases.
FREDERICH NIETZSCHE

Responsible persons are mature people who have taken charge of themselves and their conduct, who own their actions and own up to them – who answer for them.
WILLIAM JOHN BENNETT

Notes:

Daily Reflections on Life's Great Truths

June 28

Retirement is the last opportunity for individuals to reinvent themselves, let go of the past, and find peace and happiness within.
ERNIE J. ZELINSKI

Retirement, a time to enjoy all the things you never had time to do
when you worked.
CATHERINE PULSIFER

Notes:

Daily Reflections on Life's Great Truths

June 29

Better say nothing than nothing to the purpose.
ENGLISH PROVERB

I have often regretted my speech, never my silence.
PUBLILIUS SYRUS

Notes:

June 30

The ability to simplify means to eliminate the unnecessary so that the necessary may speak.
HANS HOFMANN

The essence of civilization consists not in the multiplication of wants but in their deliberate and voluntary renunciation.
MAHATMA GANDHI

Notes:

Daily Reflections on Life's Great Truths

July 1

Live a sincere life, be natural, and be honest with yourself.
MEHER BABA

In life, sincerity is always the best strategy to win people's hearts.
MEHMET MURAT ILDAN

Notes:

July 2

Sit in solitude every day. Be quiet and be still. Calm your thoughts and get to know your inner voice.
JOHN SOFORIC

Without great solitude no serious work is possible.
PABLO PICASSO

Notes:

July 3

Success seems to be connected with action.
Successful people keep moving. They make mistakes,
but they don't quit.
CONRAD HILTON

If you really want to do something, you'll find a way.
If you don't, you'll find an excuse.
JIM ROHN

Notes:

Daily Reflections on Life's Great Truths

July 4

People have only as much liberty as they have the intelligence to want and the courage to take.
EMMA GOLDMAN

Nothing is more precious than independence and liberty.
HO CHI MINH

Notes:

Daily Reflections on Life's Great Truths

July 5

Men cannot remake himself without suffering for he is both marble and the sculptor.
ALEXIS CARREL

Be still, sad heart! and cease repining; behind the clouds is the sun still shining; thy fate is the common fate of all, into each life some days must be dark and dreary.
WILLIAM WADSWORTH

Notes:

Daily Reflections on Life's Great Truths

July 6

Your talent is God's gift to you. What you do with it is your gift back to God.
LEO BUSCAGLIA

Life's greatest gift is natural talent.
P. K. THOMAJAN

Notes:

Daily Reflections on Life's Great Truths

July 7

You are today where your thoughts have brought you, you will be tomorrow where your thoughts take you.
JAMES ALLEN

If you realized how powerful your thoughts are, you would never think a negative thought.
PEACE PILGRIM

Notes:

July 8

At times it is folly to hasten; at other times, to delay. The wise do everything in its proper time.
OVID

Dost thou love life, then do not squander time, for that's the stuff life is made of.
BENJAMIN FRANKLIN

Notes:

Daily Reflections on Life's Great Truths

July
9

Tolerance is being wise enough to have no difference with those who differ from us.
PAUL CHATFIELD

Discord is the great ill of mankind; and tolerance is the only remedy for it.
VOLTAIRE

Notes:

July 10

Trust in the Lord with all thine heart; and lean not unto thine own understanding. In all ways acknowledge him, and he shall direct thy paths.
BIBLE

Let your life reflect the faith you have in God. Fear nothing and pray about everything. Be strong, trust God's word, and trust the process.
GERMANY KENT

Notes:

Daily Reflections on Life's Great Truths

July 11

The fear of the Lord is the beginning of wisdom.
BIBLE

It is the province of knowledge to speak, and it is the privilege of wisdom to listen.
OLIVER WENDELL HOLMES

Notes:

Daily Reflections on Life's Great Truths

July 12

In any given group, the most will do the least and the least the most.
MERLE P. MARTIN

It's not work, if you love what you're doing.
STEVE SEARS

Notes:

Daily Reflections on Life's Great Truths

July 13

Action makes more fortunes than caution.
VAUVENARGUES

THY actions and thy actions alone, determine thy worth.
FICHTE

Notes:

July 14

The beauty of the soul shines out when a man bears with composure one heavy mischance after another, not because he does not feel them, but because he is a man of high and heroic temper.
ARISTOTLE

Adversity is the first path to truth.
LORD BYRON

Notes:

Daily Reflections on Life's Great Truths

July 15

In the multitude of counsellors there is safety.
BIBLE

It is not often that any man can have so much knowledge of another, as is necessary to make instruction useful.
SAMUEL JOHNSON

Notes:

Daily Reflections on Life's Great Truths

July 16

An inordinate passion for pleasure is the secret of remaining young.
OSCAR WILDE

Old men for counsel, young men for action.
ADOLPH PHILIP GOUTHEY

Notes:

Daily Reflections on Life's Great Truths

July 17

A man's worth is no greater than the worth of his ambitions.
MARCUS AURELIUS

Keep away from those who try to belittle your ambitions. Small people always do that, but the really great make you believe that you, too, can become great.
MARK TWAIN

Notes:

Daily Reflections on Life's Great Truths

July 18

The greatest remedy for anger is delay.
LUCIUS ANNAEUS SENECA

If you are patient in one moment of anger, you will escape a hundred days of sorrow.
CHINESE PROVERB

Notes:

Daily Reflections on Life's Great Truths

July 19

Nothing in the affairs of men is worthy of great anxiety.
PLATO

If you want to conquer the anxiety of life, live in the moment, live in the breath.
AMIT RAY

Notes:

July 20

Beware as long as you live, of judging men by their outward appearance.
JEAN DE LA FONTAINE

Man looketh on the outward appearance, but the Lord looketh on the heart.
BIBLE

Notes:

Daily Reflections on Life's Great Truths

July 21

Next to excellence is the appreciation of it.
WILLIAM MAKESPEACE THACKERAY

Prioritize yourself. Make yourself happy and, most of all. Live, love, and appreciate what life has offered you.
WAZIM SHAW

Notes:

Daily Reflections on Life's Great Truths

July 22

Attitude is a little thing that makes a big difference.
WINSTON CHURCHILL

Your attitude will determine your success in life. You are the one who decides what type of attitude you have, it is your choice.
CATHERINE PULSIFER

Notes:

July 23

Another kind of beauty is possibly the highest type of all. Beauty of spirit, as revealed by the expression on the face of a human being. By the merry twinkle in the eye, by the smile on the lips – all indicating happiness and contentment within. This is probably the greatest beauty we will ever see.

WILLIAM ROSS

Notes:

July 24

Be glad of life because it gives you the chance to love, and to work, and to play and to look up at the stars.
HENRY VAN DYKE

To be alive, to be able to see, to walk…it's all a miracle. I have adapted the technique of living life from miracle to miracle.
ARTHUR RUBINSTEIN

Notes:

July 25

When I consider what some books have done for the world, and what they are doing, how they keep up our hope, awaken new courage and faith, soothe pain, give an ideal; life to those hours are cold and hard, bind together distant ages and foreign lands, create new worlds of beauty, bring down truth from heaven; I give eternal blessings for this gift, and thank God for books.
JAMES FREEMAN

Notes:

July 26

Business is managing risk.
LARRY JOHN PHILLIPS

Companies that grow for the sake of growth or that expand into areas outside of their core business strategy often stumble. On the other hand, companies that build scale for the benefit of their customers and shareholders more often succeed over time.
JAMIE DIMON

Notes:

Daily Reflections on Life's Great Truths

July 27

Calmness of mind is one of the beautiful jewels of wisdom. It is the result of long and patient effort in self-control. Its presence is an indication of ripened experience, and of a more than ordinary knowledge of the laws of thought.
JAMES ALLEN

Anyone can hold the helm when the sea is calm.
PUBLILIUS SYRUS

Notes:

Daily Reflections on Life's Great Truths

July 28

Nobody cares how much you know, until they know how much you care.
THEODORE ROOSEVELT

Remember that children, marriages, and flower gardens reflect the kind of care they get.
H. JACKSON BROWN, JR.

Notes:

Daily Reflections on Life's Great Truths

July 29

Give us the fortitude to endure the things which cannot be changed, and the courage to change the things which should be changed, and the wisdom to know one from the other.
BISHOP OLIVER J. HART

The only thing constant in life is change.
FRANCOIS DE LA ROCHEFOUCAULD

Notes:

Daily Reflections on Life's Great Truths

July 30

The right way is not always the popular and easy way. Standing for right when it is unpopular is a true test of moral character.
MARGARET CHASE SMITH

Nearly all men can stand adversity, but if you want to test a man's character, give him power.
ABRAHAM LINCOLN

Notes:

Daily Reflections on Life's Great Truths

July
31

Learn the sweet magic of a cheerful face.
OLIVER WENDELL HOLMES

A cheerful heart and a cheerful mind are powerful tools.
ANONYMOUS

Notes:

Daily Reflections on Life's Great Truths

August 1

This power to choose is what makes each one of us an individual, a god in his own right and our choices determine what happens to us - what our future will be - happy or unhappy, success or failure.
DAN CUSTER

As a man thinketh so is he, and as a man chooseth so is he.
RALPH WALDO EMERSON

Notes:
_____
_____
_____
_____
_____
_____
_____
_____
_____
_____
_____
_____
_____

Daily Reflections on Life's Great Truths

August 2

Extraordinary people survive under the most terrible circumstances and they become more extraordinary because of it.
ROBERTSON DAVIES

You must take personal responsibility. You cannot change the circumstances,
the seasons, or the wind, but you can change yourself. That is something you have charge of.
JIM ROHN

Notes:
_____
_____
_____
_____
_____
_____
_____
_____
_____
_____
_____
_____

August 3

Cleanliness has a powerful influence on the health and preservation of the body.
W. ASPINWALL

Nothing inspires cleanliness more than an unexpected guest.
RADHIKA MUNDRA

Notes:

Daily Reflections on Life's Great Truths

August 4

There is no exercise better for the heart than reaching down and lifting people up.
JOHN HOLMES

Sometimes it takes only one act of kindness and caring to change a person's life.
JACKIE CHAN

Notes:

Daily Reflections on Life's Great Truths

August 5

You see a lot of talented people, but you usually don't see talented people who, behind the scenes, know how to conduct themselves on a higher level.
ROMEO SANTOS

Everyone ought to bear patiently the results of his own conduct.
PHAEDRUS

Notes:

August 6

Confidence is that feeling by which the mind embarks in great and honorable courses with a sure hope and trust in itself.
MARCUS TULLIUS CICERO

No man has a right to expect others to display confidence in him if he has no confidence in himself.
ROY L. SMITH

Notes:

August 7

A good conscience is to the soul what health is to the body; it preserves a constant ease and serenity within us, and more than countervails all the calamities and afflictions that can possibly befall us.
JOSEPH ADDISON

He will easily be content and at peace, whose conscience is pure.
THOMAS A' KEMPIS

Notes:

August 8

Contentment is the philosopher's stone, which turns all it toucheth into gold; the poor man is rich with it, and the rich man is poor without it.
ELBERT HUBBARD

Enjoy your own life without comparing it with that of another.
MARIE-JEAN-ANTOINE-NICHOLAS DE CARITAT

Notes:

August 9

There is immense power when a group of people with similar interests gets together to work toward the same goals.
IDOWU KOYENIKAN

Cooperation is willing collaboration by free individuals in a collective effort that creates more value than it expends.
JAMES RAYMOND LUCAS

Notes:

Daily Reflections on Life's Great Truths

August 10

A high heart ought to bear calamities and not flee them, since in bearing them appears the grandeur of the mind and in fleeing them the cowardice of the heart.
PIETRO ARETINO

Courage is doing what you're afraid to do. There can be no courage unless you're scared.
EDDIE VERNON RICKENBACKER

Notes:

Daily Reflections on Life's Great Truths

August 11

Be courteous to all, but intimate with few, and let those few be well-tried before you give them your confidence.
GEORGE WASHINGTON

Nothing is ever lost by courtesy. It is the cheapest of the pleasures, costs nothing and conveys much. It pleases him who gives and him who receives, and thus, like mercy, it is twice blessed.
ERASTUS WIMAN

Notes:

Daily Reflections on Life's Great Truths

August 12

The desire to create is one of the deepest yearnings of the human soul.
DIETER F. UCHTDORF

Create with the heart; build with the mind.
CRISS JAMI

Notes:

August 13

Satisfaction of one's curiosity is one of the greatest sources of happiness in life.
LINUS PAULING

Much of what I stumbled into by following my curiosity an intuition turned out to be priceless later on.
STEVE JOBS

Notes:

Daily Reflections on Life's Great Truths

August 14

When it's time to die, let us not discover that we have never lived.
HENRY DAVID THOREAU

If you're afraid to die, you will not be able to live.
JAMES BALDWIN

Notes:

August 15

Nothing is more difficult, and therefore more precious, than to be able to decide.
NAPOLEON BONAPARTE

The mark of an educated man is the ability to make a reasoned guess on the basis of insufficient information.
A. L. LOWELL

Notes:

August 16

Whatever you do, do it with determination. You have one life to live; do your work with passion and give your best. Whether you want to be a chef, doctor, actor, or a mother, be passionate to get the best result.
ALIA BHATT

In all human affairs, there are efforts, and there are results, and the strength of the effort is the measure of the result.
JAMES ALLEN

Notes:

August 17

We must suffer one of two things the pain of discipline or the pain of regret and disappointment.
JIM ROHN

Personal discipline, when it becomes a way of life in our personal, family, and career lives, will enable us to do some incredible things.
ZIG ZIGLAR

Notes:

Daily Reflections on Life's Great Truths

August 18

Develop a passion for learning. If you do, you will never cease to grow.
ANTHONY J. D'ANGELO

Education is the key to unlocking the world, a passport to freedom.
OPRAH WINFREY

Notes:

August 19

Probably one of the most important lessons man has to learn is how to guide by his reason the great driving force of his emotions.
WILLIAM ROSS

Let's not forget that the little emotions are the great captains of our lives and we obey them without realizing.
VINCENT VAN GOGH

Notes:

August 20

Enthusiasm is the element of success in everything. It is the light that leads and the strength that lifts men on and up in the great struggles of scientific pursuits and of professional labor. It robs endurance of difficulty, and makes pleasure of duty.
BISHOP DOANE

In order to do great things, one must be enthusiastic.
SAINT SIMON

Notes:

August 21

We believe, as asserted in the Declaration of Independence, that all men are created equal; but that does not mean that all men are or can be equal in possessions, in ability, or in merit; it simply means that all shall stand equal in the court of law.
WILLIAM JENNINGS BRYAN

Notes:

Daily Reflections on Life's Great Truths

August 22

I have yet to meet a man as fond of high moral conduct as he is of outward appearances.
CONFUCIUS

A man without ethics is a wild beast loosed upon this world.
MANLY HALL

Notes:

August 23

The chief desire of the human race is to attain happiness. True happiness is impossible without true health. And true health is impossible without exercise.
VIC TANNY

It is remarkable how one's wits are sharpened by physical exercise.
PLINY THE YOUNGER

Notes:

Daily Reflections on Life's Great Truths

August 24

Every experience is a positive experience if I view it as an opportunity for growth and self-mastery.
BRIAN TRACY

We learn from failure, not from success.
BRAM STOKER

Notes:

Daily Reflections on Life's Great Truths

August 25

He who has faith has…an inward reservoir of courage, hope, confidence, calmness, and assuring trust that all will come out well – even though to the world, it may appear to come out most badly.
B. C. FORBES

Keep faith. The most amazing things in life tend to happen right at the moment you're about to give up hope.
ANONYMOUS

Notes:

August 26

Family and friendships are two of the greatest facilitators of happiness.
JOHN MAXWELL

Families are like branches on a tree. We grow in different directions yet our roots remain as one.
ANONYMOUS

Notes:

Daily Reflections on Life's Great Truths

August 27

Never does the human soul appear so strong as when it forgoes revenge.
EDWIN HUBBEL CHAPIN

It's one of the greatest gifts you can give yourself, to forgive. Forgive everybody.
MAYA ANGELOU

Notes:

Daily Reflections on Life's Great Truths

August 28

It's no good trying to keep up friendships. It's painful for both sides. The fact is, one grows out of people, and the only thing is to face it.
WILLIAM SOMERSET MAUGHAM

One friend in a lifetime is much; two are many; three are hardly possible.
HENRY ADAMS

Notes:

Daily Reflections on Life's Great Truths

August 29

Nobody can really guarantee the future. The best we can do is size up the chances, calculate the risks involved, estimate our ability to deal with them and then make our plans with confidence.
HENRY FORD II

What the future holds for us, depends on what we hold for the future. Hard working todays make high-winning tomorrows.
WILLIAM E. HOLLER

Notes:

Daily Reflections on Life's Great Truths

August 30

What does one person give to another? He gives of himself, of the most precious he has, he gives of his life…
ERICH FROMM

∽

Life's persistent and most urgent question is, 'What are you doing for others?'
MARTIN LUTHER KING, JR

Notes:
_____
_____
_____
_____
_____
_____
_____
_____
_____
_____
_____
_____
_____

Daily Reflections on Life's Great Truths

August 31

Use a sweet tongue, courtesy, and gentleness, and thou mayst manage to guide an elephant with a hair.
SA'DI

A gentle word, a kind look, a good-natured smile can work wonders and accomplish miracles.
WILLIAM HAZLITT

Notes:

Daily Reflections on Life's Great Truths

September

1

Gratitude is a powerful catalyst for happiness. It's the spark that lights a fire of joy in your soul.
AMY COLLETTE

∽

Gratitude is not only the greatest of virtues but the parent of all others.
MARCUS TULLIUS CICERO

Notes:

Daily Reflections on Life's Great Truths

September 2

The common denominator of success - the secret of success of every man who has ever been successful - lies in the fact that he formed the habit of doing things that failures don't like to do.
ALBERT GRAY

Habits are like a cable. We weave a strand of it every day and soon it cannot be broken.
HORACE MANN

Notes:

Daily Reflections on Life's Great Truths

September

3

Plenty of people miss their share of happiness, not because they never found it, but because they didn't stop to enjoy it.
WILLIAM FEATHER

Happiness is that pleasure which flows from the sense of virtue and from the consciousness of right deeds.
HENRY MOORE

Notes:

September 4

Heath requires healthy food.
ROGER WILLIAMS

Your body hears everything your mind says.
NAOMI JUDD

Notes:

Daily Reflections on Life's Great Truths

September

5

Home is the most popular, and will be the most enduring of all earthly establishments.
CHANNING POLLOCK

The sun at home warms better than the sun elsewhere.
ALBANIA PROVERB

Notes:

September 6

What do I get for being honest? You are getting the consciousness on your own mind that you are right. The best reward that life can bring.
ADOLPH PHILIP GOUTHEY

Whoever can be trusted with very little can also be trusted with much, and whoever is dishonest with very little will also be dishonest with much.
BIBLE

Notes:

September 7

You can be deprived of your money, your job and your home by someone else, but remember that no one can ever take away your honor.
WILLIAM LYON PHELPS

Live today and every day like a man of honor.
SAYING

Notes:

September 8

We have always held to the hope, the belief, the conviction that there is a better life, a better world, beyond the horizon.
FRANKLIN D. ROOSEVELT

Let your hopes, not your hurts, shape your future.
ROBERT SCHULLER

Notes:

September 9

Daily Reflections on Life's Great Truths

Master your craft, be nice and stay humble.
ERICK MORILLO

I stand here before you not as a prophet, but as a humble servant of you, the people.
NELSON MANDELA

Notes:

Daily Reflections on Life's Great Truths

September 10

Good humor is one of the best articles of dress one can wear in society.
WILLIAM MAKEPEACE THACKERAY

Good humor is the health of the soul; sadness is its poison.
STANISLAS

Notes:

September

11

When you hire people who are smarter than you are, you prove you are smarter than they are.
R. H. GRANT

It is better to have a fair intellect that is well-used than a powerful one that is idle.
BRYANT H. MCGILL

Notes:

Daily Reflections on Life's Great Truths

September 12

Justice is like the north star, which is fixed, and all the rest revolves about it.
CONFUCIUS

There is a higher court than courts of justice and that is the court of conscience. It supersedes all other courts.
MAHATMA GANDHI

Notes:

Daily Reflections on Life's Great Truths

September

13

Kindness is the golden chain by which society is bound together.
JAHANN WOLFGANG VON GOETHE

Kindness begins with the understanding that we all struggle.
CHARLES GLASSMAN

Notes:

Daily Reflections on Life's Great Truths

September 14

Knowledge is a comfortable and necessary retreat and shelter for us in an advanced age; and if we do not plant it while young, it will give us no shade when we grow old.
EARL OF CHESTERFIELD

'Tis not knowing much, but what is useful, that makes a wise man.
THOMAS FULLER

Notes:

Daily Reflections on Life's Great Truths

September

15

We are closer to the ants than the butterflies. Very few people can endure much leisure.
GERALD BRENAN

Only a person who can live with himself can enjoy the gift of leisure.
HENRY GREBER

Notes:

Daily Reflections on Life's Great Truths

September

16

There are only two things to aim at in life; to get what you want; and, after that, to enjoy it. Only the wisest of mankind achieve the second.
LOGAN SMITH

The way I see it, if you want the rainbow, you gotta put up with the rain.
DOLLY PARTON

Notes:

Daily Reflections on Life's Great Truths

September

17

Absence is to love what wind is to fire; it extinguishes the small, it enkindles the great.
COMTE DE BUSSY-RABUTIN

Love is shown in your deeds, not in your words.
FATHER JEROME CUMMINGS

Notes:

September

18

I entirely appreciate loyalty to one's friends, but loyalty to the cause of justice and honor stands above it.
THEODORE ROOSEVELT

∽

Never esteem anything as of advantage to you that will make you break your word or lose self-respect.
MARCUS AURELIUS

Notes:

September

19

It takes a certain level of maturity to get hit and get knocked down and get back up.
JAMAI CRAWFORD

When I can look life in the eyes, grown calm and very coldly wise, life will have given me the truth, and taken in exchange – my youth.
SARA TEASDALE

Notes:

September 20

Every single thing has a balance, and the moment we overdo that balance, something has to give, and we are punished by fate in one way or another.
LLWARD ISA

Out of moderation, pure happiness springs.
JOHANN WOLFGANG VON GOETHE

Notes:

Daily Reflections on Life's Great Truths

September 21

Do not wear yourself out to get rich; have the wisdom to show restraint.
BIBLE

Have a plan to earn money. Have a plan to carefully spend your money. Have a plan to save money. Have a plan to invest money.
ALFRED ARMAND MONTAPERT

Notes:

September 22

The right mental attitude means a great deal. A mind filled with optimistic thoughts has no room for pessimism.
E. F. GIRARD

Optimism is essential to achievement, and it is also the foundation of courage and true progress.
NICHOLAS M. BUTLER

Notes:

Daily Reflections on Life's Great Truths

September 23

Organizing is what you do before you do something so that when you do it, it is not all mixed up.
A. A. MINE

A good system shortens the road to the goal.
ORISON SWETT MARDEN

Notes:

Daily Reflections on Life's Great Truths

September
24

Our real blessings often appear to us in the shape of pains, losses, and disappointments; but let us have patience, and we soon shall see them in their proper figures.
JOSEPH ADDISON

Patient waiting is often the highest way of doing God's will.
JOHN PAYNE COLLIER

Notes:

Daily Reflections on Life's Great Truths

September

25

Do not let the behavior of others destroy your inner peace.
DALAI LAMA

Nobody can bring you peace but yourself.
RALPH WALDO EMERSON

Notes:

Daily Reflections on Life's Great Truths

September 26

Without perseverance, talent is a barren bed.
WELSH PROVERB

To persevere, trusting in what hopes he has, is courage in a man. The coward despairs.
EURIPIDES

Notes:

Daily Reflections on Life's Great Truths

September
27

There is no use whatever trying to help people who do not help themselves. You cannot push anyone up a ladder unless he be willing to climb himself.
ANDREW CARNEGIE

If we are facing in the right direction, all we have to do is keep on walking.
BUDDHIST SAYING

Notes:

Daily Reflections on Life's Great Truths

September 28

One of the many pleasures of old age is giving things up.
MALCOLM MUGGERIDGE

Throw moderation to the winds, and the greatest pleasures bring the greatest pains.
DEMOCRITUS

Notes:

Daily Reflections on Life's Great Truths

September 29

Many wealthy people are little more than the janitors of their possessions.
FRANK LLOYD WRIGHT

Of prosperity, mortals can never have enough.
AESCHYLUS

Notes:

Daily Reflections on Life's Great Truths

September 30

The man without purpose is like a ship without a rudder; a waif, a nothing, a no-man. Have a purpose in life and having it, throw such strength of mind and muscle into your work as God has given you.
THOMAS CARLYLE

The great and glorious masterpiece of man is to know how to live to purpose.
MICHEL DE MONTAIGNE

Notes:

Daily Reflections on Life's Great Truths

October 1

You can't build a reputation on what you are going to do.
HENRY FORD

A reputation for good judgement, for fair dealing, for truth, and for rectitude, is itself a fortune.
HENRY WARD BEECHER

Notes:

October 2

And the greatest lesson that mom ever taught me though was this one. She told me there would be times in your life when you have to choose between being loved and being respected. Now she said to always pick being respected.
CHRIS CHRISTIE

Respect yourself above all.
PYTHAGORAS

Notes:

Daily Reflections on Life's Great Truths

October 3

The price of greatness is responsibility.
WINSTON CHURCHILL

Few things can help an individual more than to place responsibility on him, and to let him know that you trust him.
BOOKER T. WASHINGTON

Notes:

Daily Reflections on Life's Great Truths

October 4

Retirement means doing whatever I want to do. It means choice.
DIANNE NAHIRNY

Retirement ... a time to experience a fulfilling life derived from many enjoyable and rewarding activities,
ERNIE J. ZELINSKI

Notes:

October 5

We need a reason to speak, but never to keep silent.
PIERRE NICOLE

Listen to silence. It has so much to say.
RUMI

Notes:

October 6

Truth is ever to be found in the simplicity, and not in the multiplicity and confusion of things.
ISAAC NEWTON

Simplicity is about subtracting the obvious and adding the meaningful,
JOHN MAEDA

Notes:

Daily Reflections on Life's Great Truths

October 7

Be sincere with your compliments. Most people can tell the difference between sugar and saccharine.
E. C. MCKENZIE

Sincerity is to speak as we think, to do as we pretend and profess, to perform and make good what we promise, and really to be what we would seem and appear to be.
JOHN TILLOTSON

Notes:

October 8

Solitude is not the absence of company, but the moment when our soul is free to speak to us and help us decide what to do with our lives.
PAULO COELHO

Solitude is creativity's best friend, and solitude is refreshment for our souls.
NAOMI JUDD

Notes:

Daily Reflections on Life's Great Truths

October 9

One ship drives east an another west, with the self-same winds blow; 'tis the set of the sails and not the gales that determines where they go. Like the winds of the sea are the ways of fate, as we voyage along through life; 'tis the set of the soul that decides it goal – and not the calm or strife.
ELLA WHEELER WILCOX

Notes:

Daily Reflections on Life's Great Truths

October 10

Oh, fear not in a world like this, and thou shall know erelong, know how sublime a thing it is to suffer and be strong.
HENRY WADSWORTH LONGFELLOW

In heaven above and earth below, they best can serve true gladness who meet most feelingly the calls of sadness.
WILLIAM WORDSWORTH

Notes:

October 11

Hidden talent counts for nothing.
NERO

Nature has concealed at the bottom of our minds talents and abilities of which we are not aware.
FRANCOIS DE LA ROCHEFOUCAULD

Notes:

Daily Reflections on Life's Great Truths

October 12

Sow a thought, and you reap an act; sow an act and you reap a habit; sow a habit, and you reap a character, sow a character, and you reap a destiny.
ANONYMOUS

Great thoughts come from the heart.
VAUVENARGUES

Notes:

Daily Reflections on Life's Great Truths

October
13

One realizes the full importance of time only when there is little of it left. Every man's greatest capital asset is his unexpired years of productive life.
P. W. LITCHFIELD

The bad news is time flies. The good news is you're the pilot.
MICHAEL ALTSHULER

Notes:

October 14

Since others have to tolerate my weaknesses, it is only fair that I should tolerate theirs.
WILLIAM ALLEN WHITE

Tolerant people are the happiest, so why not get rid of prejudices that hold you back.
WILLIAM MOULTON MARSTON

Notes:

October 15

The wise Man, even when he holds his Tongue, says more than the Fool when he speaks.
THOMAS FULLER

The wise does at once what the fool does at last.
BALTASAR GRACIAN

Notes:

Daily Reflections on Life's Great Truths

October 16

Most people spend most of their days doing what they do not want to in order to earn the right, at times, to do what they may desire.
JOHN MASON BROWN

∞

When work is a pleasure, life is a joy. When work is a duty, life is slavery.
MAXIM GORKY

Notes:

Daily Reflections on Life's Great Truths

October 17

I like things to happen; and if they don't happen, I like to make them happen.
WINSTON CHURCHILL

Reward of an act is to have done it.
RALPH WALDO EMERSON

Notes:

Daily Reflections on Life's Great Truths

October 18

Fire is the test of gold; adversity, of strong men.
LUCIUS ANNAEUS SENECA

Sweet are the uses of adversity, which, like the toad, ugly and venomous, wears yet a precious jewel in his head.
WILLIAM SHAKESPEARE

Notes:

October 19

A hundred sage counsels are lost upon one who cannot take advice; a hundred bits of wisdom are lost upon the unintelligent.
PANCHATANTRA

Though men give you their advice gratis, you will often be cheated if you take it.
GEORGE DENNISON PRENTICE

Notes:

October 20

Twenty years a child; twenty years running wild; twenty years a mature man – and after that, praying.
IRISH PROVERB

Probably the happiest period in life most frequently is in middle age, when the eager passions of youth are cooled and the infirmities of age not yet begun.
THOMAS ARNOLD

Notes:

Daily Reflections on Life's Great Truths

October 21

What shall it profit a man, if he shall gain the whole world, and lose his own soul?
BIBLE

No bird soars too high, if he soars with his own wings.
WILLIAM BLAKE

Notes:

Daily Reflections on Life's Great Truths

October

22

Never answer a letter while you are angry.
CHINESE PROVERB

Anger resteth in the bosom of fools.
BIBLE

Notes:

Daily Reflections on Life's Great Truths

October 23

The more you pray, the less you'll panic. The more you worship, the less you worry. You'll feel more patient and less pressured.
RICK WARREN

Worry often gives a small thing a big shadow.
SWEDISH PROVERB

Notes:

October 24

The Lord seeth not as man seeth; for man looketh on the outward appearance, but the Lord looketh on the heart.
BIBLE

They are not all saints who use holy water.
ENGLISH PROVERB

Notes:

October 25

The most impoverished people of all are those who have everything but appreciate nothing.
CRAIG D. LOUNSBROUGH

Those things you have but stupidly don't appreciate are on someone else's wish list… be grateful.
SAMIHA TOTANJI

Notes:

October 26

A positive attitude is definitely one of the keys to success. My definition of a positive attitude is a simple one: Looking for the good in all circumstances.
CATHERINE PULSIFER

It's not what happens to you, but how you react to it that matters.
EPICTETUS

Notes:

Daily Reflections on Life's Great Truths

October 27

It is amazing how complete is the delusion that beauty is goodness.
LEO TOLSTOY

Cheerfulness and contentment are great beautifiers, and are famous preservers of good looks.
CHARLES DICKENS

Notes:

October 28

Concentrate on counting your blessings and you'll have little time to count anything else.
WOODROW KROLL

Blessed are they who see beautiful things in humble places where other people see nothing.
CAMILLE PISSARRO

Notes:

Daily Reflections on Life's Great Truths

October 29

Books are the food of youth, the delight of old age; the ornament of prosperity, the refuge and comfort of adversity; a delight at home, and no hindrance abroad; companions by night, in travelling, in the country.
MARCUS TULLIUS CICERO

When we are collecting books, we are collecting happiness.
VINCENT STARRETT

Notes:

October 30

Your most unhappy customers are your greatest sources of learning.
BILL GATES

To be successful, you have to have your heart in your business, and your business in your heart.
THOMAS WATSON, SR.

Notes:

Daily Reflections on Life's Great Truths

October 31

Nothing gives a person so much advantage over another as to remain always cool and unruffled under all circumstances.
THOMAS JEFFERSON

∽

The mind is like water. When it's turbulent, it's difficult to see. When it's calm, everything becomes clear.
PRASAD MAHES

Notes:

November 1

Surround yourself with people who make you happy. People who make you laugh, who help you when you're in need. They are the ones worth keeping in your life. Everyone else is just passing through.
KARL MARX

The happiest people are those who do the most for others. The most miserable are those who do the least.
BOOKER T. WASHINGTON

Notes:

Daily Reflections on Life's Great Truths

November 2

Nothing in this world is permanent.
GERMAN PROVERB

If you do what you've always done, you'll get what you've always gotten.
ANONYMOUS

Notes:

Daily Reflections on Life's Great Truths

November

3

A good name is more desirable than great riches; to be esteemed is better than silver or gold.
BIBLE

∽

I have a dream that my four little children will one day live in a nation where they will not be judged by the color of their skin, but by the content of their character.
MARTIN LUTHER KING, JR.

Notes:

Daily Reflections on Life's Great Truths

November 4

When the mind has once formed the habit of holding cheerful happy, prosperous pictures, it will not be easy to form the opposite habit.
ORISON SWETT MARDEN

A cheerful frame of mind, reinforced by relaxation...is the medicine that puts all ghosts of fear on the run.
GEORGE MATTHEW ADAMS

Notes:

November 5

Make a choice of what you want, who you want to be and how you're going to do it. The universe will get out of the way.
WILL SMITH

You are free to choose, but the choices you make today will determine what you have, be, and do in the tomorrow of your life.
ZIG ZIGLAR

Notes:

November 6

Man is buffeted by circumstances so long as he believes himself to be the creature of outside conditions, but when he realizes that he is a creative power, and that he may command the hidden soil and seeds of his being out of which circumstances grow, he then becomes the rightful master of himself.
JAMES ALLEN

Notes:

Daily Reflections on Life's Great Truths

November 7

Compassion is the wish to see others free from suffering.
DALAI LAMA

∽

Let our hearts be stretched out in compassion toward others, for everyone is walking his or her own difficult path.
DIETER F. UCHTDORF

Notes:

November 8

A man is known by his conduct to his wife, to his family, and to those under him.
NAPOLEON BONAPARTE

Every human being has a right to be respected as a human being unless he forfeits that right by his own conduct.
MANLY HALL

Notes:

November 9

All history makes clear that an indispensable quality of any man or class that wishes to lead, to hold power and privilege in society, is boundless self-confidence.
JAMES BURNHAM

With self-confidence fulfilled, you'll find that folk have confidence in you.
JOHANN WOLFGANG VON GOETHE

Notes:

Daily Reflections on Life's Great Truths

November 10

In matters of conscience, the law of the majority has no place.
MAHTMA GANDHI

It is neither right nor safe to go against my conscience.
MARTIN LUTHER

Notes:

November 11

My crown is in my heart, not on my head; not deck's with diamonds and Indian stones, nor to be seen: my crown is called content; a crown it is that seldom kings enjoy.
WILLIAM SHAKESPEARE

Let him who has enough ask for nothing more.
HORACE

Notes:

Daily Reflections on Life's Great Truths

November 12

Alone we can do so little; together we can do so much.
HELLEN KELLER

Teamwork is the ability to work together toward a common vision. The ability to direct individual accomplishments toward organizational objectives. It is the fuel that allows common people to attain uncommon results.
ANDREW CARNEGIE

Notes:

Daily Reflections on Life's Great Truths

November 13

One ought never to turn one's back on a threatened danger and try to run away from it. If you do that, you will double the danger. But if you meet it promptly and without flinching, you will reduce the danger by half. Never run away from anything. Never!
WINSTON CHURCHILL

Only when we are no longer afraid do we begin to live.
DOROTHY THOMPSON

Notes:

Daily Reflections on Life's Great Truths

November 14

To be humble to superiors is duty, to equals courtesy, to inferiors nobleness.
BENJAMIN FRANKLIN

The small courtesies sweeten life, the greater ennoble it.
CHRISTIAN NESTELL BOVEE

Notes:

November 15

People living deeply have no fear of death.
ANAIS NIN

It hath often been said, that it is not death, but dying, which is terrible.
HENRY FIELDING

Notes:

November 16

It does not take much strength to do things, but it requires great strength to decide on what to do.
ELBERT HUBBARD

The man who insists upon seeing with perfect clearness before he decides, never decides.
HENRI FREDERIC AMIEL

Notes:

Daily Reflections on Life's Great Truths

November

17

There is nothing dependable that is not backed by character.
ROY L. SMITH

One does not need to be brilliant to be dependable.
ROY L. SMITH

Notes:

Daily Reflections on Life's Great Truths

November

18

The determination to win is the better part of winning.
DAISAKU IKEDA

Stay focused and stay determined. Don't look to anyone else to be your determination – have self-determination. It will take you very far.
JUSTICE SMITH

Notes:

November 19

Self-discipline is doing what needs to be done when it needs to be done when you don't feel like doing it.
ANONYMOUS

Discipline is just choosing between what you want now and what you want most.
ANONYMOUS

Notes:

November 20

I tell students that the opportunities I had were a result of having a good educational background. Education is what allows you to stand out.
ELLEN OCHOA

To read without reflecting is like eating without digesting.
EDMUND BURKE

Notes:

November 21

The energy that actually shapes the world springs from emotions.
GEORGE ORWELL

Man is, and was always, a block-head and dullard; much readier to feel and digest, than to think and consider.
THOMAS CARLYLE

Notes:

November 22

The successful man has enthusiasm: Good work is never done in cold blood, heat is needed to forge anything. Every great achievement is the story of a flaming heart.
A. B. ZU TAVERN

A man can succeed at almost anything for which he has unlimited enthusiasm.
CHARLES M. SCHWAB

Notes:

Daily Reflections on Life's Great Truths

November
23

I hope that we always have diversity and that we have equality and representation every step of the way.
MARSAI MARTIN

Equal rights for all, special privileges for none.
THOMAS JEFFERSON

Notes:

Daily Reflections on Life's Great Truths

November 24

Great people have great values and great ethics.
JEFFREY GITOMER

I am fully aware that everybody has a right to succeed, and success should be with ethics.
SHARAD PAWAR

Notes:

November 25

Without a proper amount of daily exercise no one can remain healthy.
ARTHUR SCHOPENHAUER

Exercise not only changes your body, it changes your mind, your attitude and your mood.
ANONYMOUS

Notes:

Daily Reflections on Life's Great Truths

November 26

View life as a continuous learning experience.
DENNIS WAITLEY

The mind once enlightened cannot again become darkened.
THOMAS PAINE

Notes:
___

November 27

An honorable man is fair even to his enemies; a dishonorable man is unfair even to his friends.
MEHMET MURAT ILDAN

Fair-minded people never twist rules for personal gain.
FRANK SONNENBERG

Notes:

November 28

Your faith can move mountains, and your doubt can create them.
ANONYMOUS

Your hardest times often lead to the greatest moments of your life. Keep the faith. It will all be worth it in the end.
ANONYMOUS

Notes:

Daily Reflections on Life's Great Truths

November
29

An ounce of blood is worth more than a pound of friendship.
SPANISH PROVERB

Family means nobody gets left behind or forgotten.
DAVID OGDEN STIERS

Notes:

Daily Reflections on Life's Great Truths

November 30

The weak can never forgive. Forgiveness is the attribute of the strong.
MAHATMA GANDHI

It's not an easy journey, to get to a place where you forgive people. But it is such a powerful place, because it frees you.
TYLER PERRY

Notes:

Daily Reflections on Life's Great Truths

December

1

One loyal friend is worth ten thousand relatives.
EURIPIDES

The firmest friendships have been formed in mutual adversity, as iron is most strongly united by the fiercest flame.
CHARLES CALEB COLTON

Notes:

December 2

The way to wealth is as plain as the way to market. It depends on two words, industry and frugality: that is, waste neither time nor money, but make the best use of both. Without industry and frugality, nothing will do, and with them, everything.
BENJAMIN FRANKLIN

Notes:

December 3

Taking satisfies you. Giving satisfies two.
MAXINE LAGACE

Your path to greatness starts the moment you find the courage to reach out with generosity.
KEITH FERRAZZI

Notes:

Daily Reflections on Life's Great Truths

December 4

Be gentle with your words – you can't take them back.
WILLIE NELSON

An able man shows his spirit by gentle words and resolute actions.
EARL OF CHESTERFIELD

Notes:

Daily Reflections on Life's Great Truths

December 5

Gratitude helps you to grow and expand; gratitude brings joy and laughter into your life and into the lives of all those around you.
EILEEN CADDY

There is a calmness to a life lived in gratitude, a quiet joy.
RALPH H. BLUM

Notes:

Daily Reflections on Life's Great Truths

December 6

True happiness is...to enjoy the presence, without anxious dependence upon the future.
LUCIUS ANNAEUS SENECA

The moments of happiness we enjoy take us by surprise. It is not that we seize them, but that they seize us.
ASHLEY MONTAGU

Notes:

Daily Reflections on Life's Great Truths

December 7

It is certain that tis easier to preserve Health than to recover it, and to prevent Diseases than to cure them.
DR. GEORGE CHEYNE

Look to your health; and if you have it, praise God, and value it next to a good conscience; for health is the second blessing that we mortals are capable of; a blessing that money cannot buy.
IZAAK WALTON

Notes:

December 8

Seek home for rest, for home is best.
THOMAS TUSSER

Home sweet home. This is the place to find happiness. If one doesn't find it here, one doesn't find it anywhere.
M. K. SONI

Notes:

December 9

An honest heart possesses a kingdom.
LUCIUS ANNAEUS SENECA

For he who is honest is noble, whatever his fortunes or birth.
CARY

Notes:

Daily Reflections on Life's Great Truths

December 10

He has honor if he holds himself to an ideal of conduct though it is inconvenient, unprofitable, or dangerous to do so.
WALTER LIPPMANN

My honor is dearer to me than my life.
MIGUEL DE CERVANTES

Notes:

December 11

Hope Is being able to see that there is a light despite all the darkness.
DESMOND TUTU

Hope is outreaching desire with expectancy of good. It is characteristic of all living beings.
EDWARD S. AME

Notes:

Daily Reflections on Life's Great Truths

December
12

Self-praise is for losers. Be a winner. Stand for something. Always have class, and be humble.
JOHN MADDEN

Talent is God-given. Be humble. Fame is man-given. Be grateful. Conceit is self-given. Be careful.
HARVEY MACKAY

Notes:

Daily Reflections on Life's Great Truths

December

13

Mirth is like a flash of lighting, that breaks through a gloom of clouds, and glitters for a moment; cheerfulness keeps up a kind of daylight in the mind, and fills it with a steady and perpetual serenity.
JOSEPH ADDISON

It is the ability to take a joke, not make one, that proves you have a sense of humor.
MAX EASTMAN

Notes:

Daily Reflections on Life's Great Truths

December 14

It is not enough to have a good mind; the main thing is to use it well.
RENE DESCARTES

To the dull mind, all nature is leaden. To the illumined mind, the whole world burns and sparkles with light.
RALPH WALDO EMERSON

Notes:

Daily Reflections on Life's Great Truths

December 15

Justice will not condemn even the Devil himself wrongfully.
THOMAS FULLER

The triumph of justice is the only peace.
ROBERT GREEN INGERSOLL

Notes:

Daily Reflections on Life's Great Truths

December 16

You can accomplish by kindness what you cannot by force.
PUBLILIUS SYRUS

When words are both true and kind, they can change the world.
BUDDHA

Notes:
_____
_____
_____
_____
_____
_____
_____
_____
_____
_____
_____
_____

December 17

Without knowledge, action is useless, and knowledge without action is futile.
ABU BAKR

Risk comes from not knowing what you're doing.
WARREN BUFFETT

Notes:

Daily Reflections on Life's Great Truths

December

18

If you are losing your leisure, look out; you may be losing your soul.
LOGAN PEARSALL SMITH

They talk of the dignity of work. The dignity is in leisure.
HERMAN MELVILLE

Notes:

Daily Reflections on Life's Great Truths

December 19

Life is a succession of lessons which must be lived to be understood.
HELEN KELLER

Don't settle for what life gives you; make life better and build something.
ASHTON KUTCHER

Notes:
___

Daily Reflections on Life's Great Truths

December 20

Do not rebuke an older man harshly, but exhort him as if he were your father. Treat younger men as brothers, older women as mothers, and younger women as sisters, with absolute purity.
BIBLE

Who are wise in love, love most, say least.
ALFRED TENNYSON

Notes:

December 21

A truly great book should be read in youth, again in maturity and once more in old age, as a fine building should be seen by morning light, at noon and by moonlight.
ROBERTSON DAVIES

As I grow older, I pay less attention to what men say, I just watch what they do.
ANDREW CARNEGIE

Notes:

Daily Reflections on Life's Great Truths

December 22

Pleasures are enhanced that are sparingly enjoyed.
JUVENAL

Moderation is the key of lasting enjoyment.
HOSEA BALLOU

Notes:

December 23

It is neither wealth nor splendor, but tranquility and occupation, which give happiness.
THOMAS JEFFERSON

It is not large funds that are wanted, but a constant supply, like a small stream that never dies. To have a great capital is not so necessary as to know how to manage a small one and never be without a little.
WILLIAM COOPER

Notes:

December 24

Optimism is a happiness magnet. If you stay positive, good things and good people will be drawn to you.
MARY LOU RETTON

Optimism inspires, energizes, and brings out our best. It points the mind toward possibilities and helps us think creatively past problems.
PRICE PRITCHETT

Notes:

December 25

Rush is the enemy of growth. Leaf by leaf, the great oak grows into a sturdy tree. Forty years alone in the desert produced a Moses. Three years alone in the Arabian desert perfected Paul's vision and thought, made him a world citizen.
ADOLPH PHILIP GOUTHEY

He that can have patience, can have what he will.
BENJAMIN FRANKLIN

Notes:

Daily Reflections on Life's Great Truths

December 26

This is the gift that God reserves for his special proteges, talent and beauty he gives to many. Wealth is commonplace, fame not rare. But peace of mind – that is his final guerdon of approval, the fondest sign of his love. He bestows it. Most men are never blessed with it, others wait all their lives – yes, far into advanced age – for this gift to descend upon them.
JOSHUA LIEBMAN

Notes:

Daily Reflections on Life's Great Truths

December 27

Genius is perseverance in disguise.
MIKE NEWLIN

All the performances of human art, at which we look with praise or wonder, are instances of the resistless force of perseverance.
SAMUEL JOHNSON

Notes:

Daily Reflections on Life's Great Truths

December
28

There aren't any great men. There are just great challenges that ordinary men like you and me are forced by circumstances to meet.
WILLIAM F. HALSEY

∽

There is no failure except in no longer trying. There is no defeat except from within, no really insurmountable barrier save our own inherent weakness of purpose.
KIN HUBBARD

Notes:

December 29

It is best to be moderate in all things including material possessions.
LARRY JOHN PHILLIPS

When you lose your desire for things that do not matter you will be free.
MORIHEI UESHIBA

Notes:

Daily Reflections on Life's Great Truths

December

30

We all have a purpose in life, and when you find yours you will recognize it.
CATHERINE PULSIFER

Your purpose in life is to find your purpose and give your whole heart and soul to it.
BUDDAH

Notes:

December 31

Associate yourself with men of good quality if you esteem your own reputation; for 'tis better to be alone than in bad company.
GEORGE WASHINGTON

If I take care of my character, my reputation will take care of me.
DWIGHT L. MOODY

Notes:

About the Author

Born and raised in northeastern Indiana, Larry John Phillips is married with 2 children and 5 grandchildren. He is a semi-retired business owner with a B.S. degree from Purdue University. During his free time, in addition to collecting quotations, Larry enjoys playing golf, gardening and spending time at their lake cottage with family.

During the last 40 years, Larry collected quotations on different topics and formed a habit of reflecting on them as part of his morning routine. Over the years he continued to expand the collection of his favorite quotations and today it consists of over 100 topics and 2,500 quotations. The journey with quotations has had a profound, uplifting, and thought-provoking impact on his life.

Progressive Rising Phoenix Press is an independent publisher. We offer wholesale pricing and multiple binding options with no minimum purchases for schools, libraries, book clubs, and retail vendors. We offer substantial discounts on bulk orders and discounts on individual sales through our online store. Please visit our website at:

www.ProgressiveRisingPhoenix.com

*If you enjoyed reading this book, please
review it on Amazon, B & N, or Goodreads.
Thank you in advance!*

Milton Keynes UK
Ingram Content Group UK Ltd.
UKHW050959291024
450401UK00009B/176